Caught Up & Called Out

BRANDON BAUMGARTEN

"BRINGING OUT THE LEADER IN YOU"

authorHOUSE®

AuthorHouse™
1663 Liberty Drive
Bloomington, IN 47403
www.authorhouse.com
Phone: 1 (800) 839-8640

Published by AuthorHouse   11/03/2015

ISBN: 978-1-5049-5474-7 (sc)
ISBN: 978-1-5049-5475-4 (e)

Library of Congress Control Number: 2015916390

Print information available on the last page.

Foreword

By Rhett Laubach

I WAS SKEPTICAL ....when my friend Brandon Baumgarten told me he wrote a book. I was skeptical for three reasons:

1. Brandon is a good man, but he is still a young man in his early twenties.
2. Over the past twenty years I have read too many books written by twenty-somethings that lacked a strong message and quality writing. They just felt like glorified business cards.
3. I've delivered leadership and life skills keynotes and workshops since 1991. It is sometimes challenging for me to stumble on content that feels new, relevant and insightful.

Simply put, I am skeptical no more. Caught Up and Called Out is a great piece of work. If you are seeking a book that entertains, inspires and provides meaningful and tangible content on how to step up and lead with purpose and passion, then stop reading this foreword, turn the page and get to work. What Brandon has done here is weave together a collection of engaging stories, insightful questions and lessons crafted in a language that feels fresh, personal and motivating.

I've known Brandon for a number of years. I've watched him grow as a young student leader in the Oklahoma FFA Association (www.okffa.org). I am proud of the work he has created for you. Ever since I started reading books like this when I was in middle school, starting with Zig Ziglar's See You At The Top, I knew it was worth my time when the margins filled with my own ideas of lessons to teach in my programs that were inspired by the author's content. Caught Up and Called Out has very few blank margins. Brandon challenges you to activate your leadership even when it's not the comfortable course of action. You are going to learn about the power of focusing on being available to others and to not miss opportunities to impact lives. Brandon teaches the true power of true leadership. In chapter six you will be called to consider how "selflessness breeds restoration". You were certainly created to make a positive difference in the lives of others. Caught Up and Called Out is designed to show you how to strengthen the muscles necessary to do just that.

My favorite part of Caught Up and Called Out is the knowledge that Brandon lives what he writes. Brandon is a strong, Christian man who lives with conviction. His daily actions are simply reflections of his Christ-like character, positive focus, strong work-ethic and desire to serve others. Keep this book close. It will serve to inform, challenge and motivate you for many years to come.

Respectfully,

Rhett Laubach

Professional Speaker/Trainer/Author, Leadership

Expert, Presentation Skills Coach

Owner, YourNextSpeaker, LLC

Preface

Do you ever feel like your life gets super busy? We have all been there at some point in our lives where time simply escapes us because of the constant demands of our daily schedules. Simply put: we get caught up in our own plans, calendars, agendas, that it often becomes easy to forget about our purpose in life. I know it has happened to me on many different occasions. Let me share with you one of these times.

One day I was driving to town and to avoid the construction of town, I decided to be like Rodney Atkins and "Take a Back Road". I notice that there were no cars, no traffic, and no construction. Feeling good about life, I then crank up the radio to listen to hear some wise financial words from money expert, Dave Ramsey. Life couldn't be better!

As I'm listening to some great commentary and driving down this traffic-less road, I begin to zone into my own little world and forgot about everything around me. Before you know it, Dave Ramsey is talking about one of my favorite financial topics on the radio about how to plan for retirement while in college. At this point, my mental juices are flowing, getting so caught up in the moment, I'm driving and then, all of a sudden, I blow right past a stop sign without even thinking. What was even worse was that a police officer was right there at the intersection of where I crossed. As soon as I did this, I looked behind me and saw red and blue lights. I pulled my car over and talked with the police officer about what I did wrong, admitting that I was guilty as charged. He said to me, "Mr. Baumgarten, I pulled you over because you didn't stop at the stop sign. In the future you need to make sure you stop, look both ways, consider other traffic, and then proceed with caution." He gave me a warning and we both went our separate ways and even though I did violate a traffic law, the officer did his job greatly and made me thankful for the awesome police officers that we have in our country.

As I went on with my day, I couldn't help but think of what I had learned from this event. You see, often times we get caught up in the business of life, the fast lane of life if you will, and forget to stop, look around and consider others who might come our way. In our daily lives, we must be willing to yield to what's important, for if we don't, it could be costly, not in just terms of a ticket, but in terms of time and opportunity. In this life, I don't want for one second to miss out on what's important. I don't want to get so caught up in the world of "ME", that I forget about the universe of everyone else. Each one of us was called to serve a very special purpose, but if we don't take the time out to STOP and discover that important purpose, then how will we ever fulfill it? In this life, I don't want to roll passed any opportunity, any chance to change a life, or any purpose that I've been meant to live out.

Sure, it's easy to get distracted, but we must remember to stay the course. We must stop, look around, consider those who are around us, and then proceed with life, seeking out opportunities to serve and being aware of the positive impact we can make. Now, more than ever we need leaders to rise up and take a stand, people who are CAUGHT UP in the pursuit of impacting their surroundings and CALLED OUT to fulfill the purpose you have been destined to live up every day. May this book help you realize that very important purpose as a call to action in your life.

No one regardless of their age, background, hometown, mistakes, successes, or any other factor, can escape the profound truth that they were born to live a life of meaning and impact. This book was not written to impress you, but to inspire you to be all that you can be. As you read this book, my ultimate hope is that you realize the calling of leadership, the unwavering purpose within your life and understand that you have an influence the world is anxiously waiting to see. Its time to bring out the leader in you!

Lead On!

Brandon Baumgarten

Chapter 1

Introduction

T he lights were dimmed, the cameras were rolling, the crowd was silent, and the anticipation in the room was building. Emotion, fatigue, excitement, and nervousness were just some of the many feelings I was experiencing in these final minutes. I had spent the entire week in Louisville, Kentucky attending the National FFA Convention representing the state of Oklahoma as a National Officer Candidate. This convention is the annual highlight of the National FFA Organization (formerly known as the Future Farmers of America) and is one of the largest conventions in the United States. There were 43 of us candidates total who had been interviewing tirelessly throughout the week, only 6 of us would be elected to serve. Finally, the moment we had all been waiting for had come upon us as the new National FFA Officer Team was to be announced in front of an arena filled with over sixty-thousand people.

For months, each of us candidates had been training rigorously with leadership coaches, interview experts, and public speaking professionals. I had poured my heart into my development, striving to make the most of every opportunity, training, and resource I could possibly get ahold of. If selected to be on the National Officer Team, you would become an ambassador for over a half-million members and leading the largest student-led organization in the world. The stakes were high and everything that could have been done to prepare and perform was done. All that remained, was the announcement of the new team.

"Breathe in, breathe out. Breathe in, breathe out. Don't be nervous, if it's meant to be it will happen." These were the expressions and words I kept telling myself as I stood in the row with all of the other candidates. We had formed a bond of friendship as we had trained over the months, and we cherished the memories we had made.

All of a sudden one of the selection committee members stepped up to the microphone and said, "Mr. President, I have a list of names, we the committee, would like to recommend to the delegates for your new National FFA Officer Team." She proceeded to read the names starting with the 4 region vice presidents. One by one the candidates who had been selected as a Region Vice-President rushed onto the stage in celebration. After they went through the offices of vice-presidents and secretary, there remained one final office left, the office of National FFA President. My name had yet to be called, and I had never been more nervous in my life. As they were about to announce the final office, I then closed my eyes, and took a deep breath, thinking to myself, "Will they call my name?!" The committee member then said, "And Your New National FFA President........FROM THE STATE OF.............VIRGINIA!"

Immediately, I was struck with a combination of emotions. I was so happy and excited for my friends who had been elected. However, I could not help but feel like I was a failure. I felt like I had failed my parents, my friends, my state, my teachers, everybody who had supported me, I felt like I had let them down. For the next few days, I was completely CAUGHT UP in the idea that I was a failure and in my mind, nothing could change that. However, even though my name was never called on stage to be a National FFA Officer, could it have been that my name was being CALLED OUT to serve an entirely different purpose?

After returning home from the National FFA Convention, I came back wishing to put my training and skills learned to the same cause of impacting others, but instead through the realm of professional speaking and workshop presenting. At that point, I did not know where to go or how to start, but people began to speak into my dreams and got behind me once again.

There is no way in the world I would be doing what I am doing today if it wasn't for the mentors, teachers, & fellow speakers who have helped me along the way. I have to admit I still get a little nervous from time to time, but I love every minute of it. I wish I could tell you about all the stories I've witnessed. I wish I could describe to you all the tears of inspiration I have seen. I wish I could articulate to you the warmth of a hug from a student who discovered his self-worth again. When you get to see students fully engaged, when you get to see depressed adults truly encouraged, when you get to see people actively empowered to be the person they are meant to be, that my friends, is worth everything in the world. The point is sometimes when we think we have lost everything and become completely caught up in our failure, it may just be that we are being called out to achieve something greater. As leaders, it is easy for us to be caught up in our own failures, disappointments, obstacles, drama, and often times, it seems like we are in our own little world.

In this book, we will explore 6 areas of leadership which I believe best bring out the leader in us. These areas are availability, authenticity, adventure, ambassadorship, acknowledgement, and abandoning self. As you read through this book, I want you to keep in mind these three specific words: Engage, Encourage, Empower. Here is the meaning:

ENGAGE: Get Others Involved
ENCOURAGE: Make Others Feel Their Worth
EMPOWER: Give Others the Motivation to Do Something.
These are my "3 Es of Leadership Analysis", I believe every leader needs to have in check mentally. Read this book with this mental approach, "How can I use this material to engage others? How can I use this content to encourage

others? How can I use this message to empower others?" Asking yourself these questions while reading will help you better understand the content as well as help develop your leadership mindset.

For the past two years, I have been documenting, recording, and compiling my personal leadership experiences into my blogs, social media sites, and journals. In this book, I have combined them all into one giant piece while pouring out my heart and soul into this text. My hope is you will not read this book as just another leadership resource; instead, I hope you will read it as a transcript of my heart from one developing leader to another. Although I am seeking a bachelor's degree in leadership, and have had many positive experiences in several roles of leadership, I will be the first to tell you that I do not know everything about leadership, but what I do know is that everyone is affected by it. Everyone is called to lead in their own special way and you can play a big part in leaving a personal positive impact on this world. Let this book not just be another book, but a tool you can use to bring forth the leader in you who leaves an impact on us. As you read this book, I challenge you to become the leader who is caught up in the pursuit of an impact and called out to fulfill the destiny you were born to achieve.

CAUGHT UP: How can you bring out the leader in others?

CALLED OUT: Describe a time you failed at something and had to move on, what did you learn from this experience and how did you grow?

What Do You Think?

_____

_____

_____

_____

_____

_____

_____

Chapter 2

Availability:
"ARE YOU OPEN?"

T hey say that the greatest leader isn't the one who has the most abilities, but the one who has the most availability to serve others. Being available is the starting point for every servant leader, because if we are not available to serving others, if we are not open to reaching out to others or welcoming to learning through new experiences, then this idea of making an impact is just wishful thinking. Abilities are tremendous assets to have in your leadership repertoire, but they are null and void until we become available to use them to serve others.

Have you ever hopped in the car to go shopping at your favorite store only to find that the store is closed when you arrive? This has happened to me on more than just one occasion and quite honestly, when it happens I get kind of bummed out. The reason being is because I am normally looking forward to getting something I want out of that store, but when it's closed, I get nothing. The store may have all the goods, best deals, services, and items that I could ever want, but at this time, the products, functions, and abilities of that store are completely useless to me, because it's not open, it's not available, it's closed.

Unfortunately, there is a striking relationship between this analogy and the state of the current leaders of this millennial generation. Too many leaders have the goods, talents, and abilities to lead and serve others. These leaders have all it takes to truly benefit their schools, communities, and world, but instead, they get caught up in their own little world of abilities, focusing on what they have to offer, rather than what they are willing to give and who they are willing to help. By this merit, they choose not to be open to others, they choose to be unavailable to serve; thus, putting a closed sign on their impact. Ask yourself while reading, "Am I Open to Serve?" We must focus on availability rather than just our abilities.

However, when looking at our world, it's easy to conclude that we focus on the abilities alone. We focus on who can break Michael Jordan's shooting record the fastest. Who will be the next winner of The Voice? Who will win the College Football Playoff? Who will win the next Presidential Election?

Case in point, our society is consumed with the concept of abilities and although it's great to possess them, a question we should be asking is, "What will we do with them?" Abilities say, "This is what I can do." Availability says, "This is what I am willing to do." It's so easy to have the ability to do something, but it's a whole other matter entirely to be available to do it.

They say that the people who gain the most from Black Friday are the ones who sit back and watch the other shoppers. If you ever want to see some funny stuff, sit back and watch the customers shopping at Wal-Mart on Black Friday. To say the least, "It is a Hoot!" One minute it looks like shoppers are doing their own reenactment of the "Running of the Bulls" event as they race to get into the store and then the next minute it looks like shoppers are trying to play football through the shopping aisles, where the product item is the football, the other shoppers are the blockers, and the checkout line is the end zone. People both young and old are involved in Black Friday and some shop at much different speeds than others. But the philosophy that many shoppers seem to keep in mind, reminds me of a line from the movie "The Lion King", where Nala said to Simba "You Gotta Mufasa!" To put it simply, Black Friday is a crazy day.

Now, the last time I went to shop on Black Friday, it was around 2:30 in the afternoon, at that point I had missed most of the chaos, so I thought. However, Wal-Mart was just as packed and flooded with people as it was at the crack of dawn. I couldn't help but stand in shock as I saw items fly off the wall left and right. I felt horrible for the boy who was stocking the aisles, because he sure had his work cut out. Needless to say, people were completely caught up in the moment, doing everything they could to get a great deal.

In the midst of the craziness of the crowds, something caught my attention. As everyone was busy getting their items, I noticed that there was an elderly lady walking through the aisles and asking different ones, "How may I help you?" She was a Wal-Mart employee, where she served as the part-time Greeter and was a 30 year veteran of the store based upon the 30 year button she proudly wore, but on this day she was taking her job to a whole new level. My heart was touched as I watched this elderly woman reach out to others and show genuine concern for every customer she met. Her passion for her job was evident and she absolutely enjoyed what she did and she did not miss a single beat. She was a true light in the midst of Black Friday.

Her question of "How May I Help You?" is what stuck with me the most. Back in the day, before Wal-Mart transitioned to the Super-Center style it is today, the employees use to wear blue vests that would say on the back in bright bold lettering: "How May I Help You?" This vest signified that they were there to help you find what you needed.

You see, this is 1 of 3 questions that everyone needs to be asking others, "How May I Help You? "How May I Serve You?", and "How May I Get Involved?" It's the secret question to becoming a servant leader. We were created to be helpful in a helpless world. We were made to make a difference. The scary thing is you and I have the chance to help others in ways we may not even realize. By healthy decision-making and keeping our priorities in check, we can help a world that greatly stands in need of help. Helping our world starts by getting involved and one main reason we have a lack of help is because we have a lack of involvement in our world. Here are some lack of involvement scenarios.

Today, you don't have to look far to see new trends and statistics released by schools that show parental participation in parent-teacher conferences are drastically declining. Parent-teacher conferences are great opportunities for parents to communicate with their child's teacher and help advocate for their child's future. We can definitely HELP our world through education.

According to the United States Election Projection Council, 36.4% of eligible American voters actually voted in the 2014 midterm election. This was the lowest voter turnout since WWII. We live in the greatest nation in the world, because of the freedoms we have. Every person has a voice and a right to help choose what path our country will take. We can HELP our world through civics.

According to the Hartford Institute of Religion Research, 40% of Americans claim they attend church weekly, however, church numbers show that less than 20% of Americans actually attend services. As a preacher's kid, I've pretty much grown up in the church, through that, I've learned that the church isn't limited to a building, church is community. As servant leaders we have a moral responsibility to reach out to others in our community and help better others. We were not meant to hide our hope, we were meant to share it. We can HELP our world through the sharing of our hope.

Now, here is a statistic on prominent involvement. According to the Syracuse Review, over 140.1 million people participated in Black Friday and Thanksgiving weekend sales in 2014.

This shows that it is evident that we have the people to get involved and help our world, but it all boils down to a matter of choice. What is most important to us? Material things pass away, but impact will forever remain. We can buy all the items in Wal-Mart, we can have all the latest apps on our iPhones, but at the end of the day, it still won't make us happy.

The need for leaders to rise up has never been more prevalent than today. Our world needs people who are willing to stand out from the crowd and stand up to HELP the future. In the midst of the crowd, this Wal-Mart greeter stood out, because she dared to do the uncommon thing. Our World is craving for a change that can only be born from the boldness of servant leaders. We need leaders who are not afraid to be available to lead. It's time to ask a helpless world, "How May I Help You?" We must be people who will seek to take a stand in pursuit of the greater good. No matter how dark our world may get, we each can shine our light on this globe just like the greeter at Wal-Mart who portrayed her availability in an impactful way. Are You Ready to HELP our World? Are you willing to be available? Its starts by asking 3 simple questions, "How May I HELP You?" "How May I Serve You?" and "How May I Get Involved?" Strive to be the leader who is open for service and available to lead.

CAUGHT UP: Ask yourself, "What attributes will make me stand out from the crowd?"

CALLED OUT: Tell us a time when you were willing to help someone else, what was the result of this action?

What Do You Think?

_____

_____

_____

_____

_____

_____

_____

Chapter 3

Authenticity:
GET REAL

Recently, I had a friend of mine challenge me to try to do something random, to get out of the norm, to dare to be different, and break through the monotony of everyday life. This challenge has caused me to really focus and pay attention to the little things in life; it's made me become more aware of my surroundings and the people around me. So, with this challenge in mind, I visited Burger King for lunch on the road this past year, I don't normally like going through the drive thru, because you don't get to meet as many people as you do inside. As you can tell, I'm an extrovert!

When I walked into Burger King, there were indeed A LOT of people there, standing in 3 lines waiting for their orders to be taken, it was definitely a lunch rush hour. I hopped in line, waiting for my order to be taken. As I waited, I couldn't help but notice a mom and her younger son ordering in the front, the boy was pleading for a chicken nugget kids' meal, but the Mom said, "No". Having to explain, she looked at her 6-year old son and said, "Honey, those chicken nuggets don't have the real chicken in it, its artificial stuff. You want the real stuff, because it can help you grow stronger and it will be healthier for you." Now, as I heard this conversation, I thought, "Wow, this mom just made a great point." Not only in terms of setting healthy eating habits for her son, but also from a leadership perspective. You see, a lot of times in life we settle for the artificial stuff, sometimes we have artificial chocolate, artificial attitudes, artificial friends, and sadly, many times we can tend to live artificial lives.

If we want to desire to be effective servant leaders, then we cannot allow ourselves to be fake. Reality is that too many people have already resolved to live with a counterfeit attitude. Think about how much you will stand out from the pack, when you choose to be genuine in your actions, words, social media posts, and altogether in your life. You will begin to fill a void that so many people are longing to fill.

The need for authentic leaders is so massive, that I believe when authenticity comes alive in you, it will bring others to life as well. Activate the people around you by showing them what it means to get real. It's a wakeup call that is both refreshing and stimulating to a world that has been lulled to sleep by the mediocrity and artificiality of poor decision making. Just like the mom at Burger King, we cannot be satisfied with the imitations. I don't know about you, but I desire the "Real Stuff". We were not meant to be artificial, we were meant to be authentic. We must choose to **Get Real**.

Getting real starts by realizing who you are and taking time to really examine what your life portrays. I have condensed the rest of this chapter into 3 "**Get Real**" questions each of us should ask ourselves. These questions can help you dive deep into your authentic identity as well as help you understand the importance of staying true to one's self.

The first question is, "**Who am I?**" In this question, think about all the things that make you who you are. Your likes and dislikes, the people in your family, your friends, habits, dreams, faith, ambitions, goals, favorite sports teams, etc. When I first thought about answering these questions I began to focus on each for one week at a time. This allowed me to explore who I was and helped me to develop a natural self-confidence. It cleared up so much in my life where I could confidently see my goals, purpose, and passion. The value of knowing who you are is priceless because it helps you get a better grasp of the person you truly are and a clearer picture of your own identity.

The second question you need to ask is, "**What do I stand for?**" This question is one that should articulate the values, morals, and fundamentals you hold dear to your heart. If someone was to look at your life right now what would they see you living for? If someone took a glance at your Facebook, Twitter, or Instagram accounts what kind of message would they see? The things we stand for in life add so much to what people remember us by and the legacies we leave behind. As a servant leader, the need to take proactive stands is critical to paving the way for the future. Because if we refuse to take a stand for others to follow then we cannot complete the purpose every leader was called out to fulfill. Discovering what you authentically stand for as a leader will help you get real.

The final question of authenticity that each of us need to ask is, "**Where am I going**?" Many leaders are stuck in a state of confusion where they don't know who they are, they can't understand what they stand for, which results in a blurred vision of where they are going. The bottom-line is once we understand who we are and what we stand for; we can better determine where we are going. Servant leaders are compelled to live these critical ideals out.

Get a hold of this question: Did you know that there are people who are waiting to be touched by the real you? Furthermore, when we become real with ourselves, we can become more real with others. We can impact others through the authenticity of our lives because our authenticity was created for a purpose and it's nothing to be ashamed of.

Sure, the world shows us many artificial things which may appear attractive just like those chicken nuggets at Burger King, but at the end of the day, authenticity is what counts, because it portrays quality, uniqueness, sincerity, and most importantly, is the best way for us to live. When we choose to "Get Real" and discover who we really are, we will grow into better individuals and more effective leaders. For every leader in this world, we can no longer afford to be imitations of impact, there are too many lives at stake who need to see the real you.

Authenticity has called us out for a reason, and it's time that we answer the call. No one in this entire world, past, present, or future will ever be the same as you nor will they be able to make the impact that you can make, so why not be the best "You" that you can be? It all starts by being original, it starts by being authentic. It just goes to show you how many leadership lessons we can actually learn from a boy, a mom, and a simple chicken nuggets kid's meal. Now that's what I call "Food 4 Thought". Be Authentic!

Caught Up: Do you consider yourself to be an authentic leader?

Called Out: What are some ways you might be able to apply authenticity to your daily life? Ask yourself the 3 "Get Real" questions to discover the real you.

What Do You Think?

_____

_____

_____

_____

_____

_____

_____

_____

Chapter 4

Adventurous:
LEADING FEARLESSLY

Even though I am 22, I can honestly say I'm not the biggest Taylor Swift fan on the planet, however, when you have a 9 year old sister, you can't help but hear Miss Swift quoted day after day. In fact, I've often found myself applying some of her song titles to certain situations. For example, I've been in a welding shop and seen "Sparks Fly" and in my opinion, there are many politicians in Washington who "Should've Said No" on many different bills, but that's for another day.

However, there was one particular time when one of Taylor Swift's song titles became more real to me than ever before. A few months ago I met my family in Branson, MO for a quick weekend vacation. It was a blast and after five years, it was well overdue. The first day we arrived in Branson, we settled into our hotel room, and like a fish out of water, my little sister immediately grabbed me and together we went after the swimming pool.

As soon as we got there, my sister got in the shallow side and was content in staying there. While she was there, I ran and jumped into the deep end of the pool. She was ecstatic to see my big splash and yelled out a big, "Wow!!" She then hopped on the edge, ran and jumped into the shallow end, and made a big splash of her own. She loved it!! She continued to jump into the same spot in the pool time after time. However, I could see in her eyes, that she craved to do something more. I asked her if she wanted to make an even bigger splash, an emphatic "Yes!!" she replied. "Okay," I said, "then come jump in the deep section, I'll be there to catch you." As soon as I said this, her enthusiasm went from high to low; she then hung her head, and responded in a quiet voice saying, "No, I don't think I can do that Brandon. I've never been down there before."

I told her she could make the jump if she wanted to and assured her that I'd be there to make sure she was safe. After I said this, she got out of the pool and walked over to the deep end and looked down. She said, "Ok Brandon, I'm going to jump." She then counted to 2, stepped back, and said, "I think I'm going to go back to the shallow end." Again and again, she would go to the deep end to jump and never would do it. Finally, I said, "Sister, you can make the jump, you just got to believe in yourself."

"Okay," she said. She then sat down, thought for a while, and before I know it, she gets up, takes a deep breath, closes her little eyes, begins to run, and JUMPS INTO THE DEEP!

She emerged her head up from the water, gasped her breath, and was so excited! I was so proud of her! She got back up and started jumping over and over again into the deep section. You could not have stopped her and all of a sudden Taylor Swift's song "Fearless" popped into my head. Because that day my sister had proved that she was bigger than her fear, and became every bit of the word-"Fearless".

This memorable story reveals to me a common denominator in the lives of every leader. The fact is we all have things in our own lives that we consider as obstacles, fear factors, things that are holding us back from where we need to be. Many of us are swimming in the shallow, when we should be diving in the deep. We may think we are in over our heads, but the truth is we are only as in over heads as much as allow our heads to be under water. We have a choice: to live with fear or to live fearlessly. The question is, "How will we live?" Your life is bigger than your fear and it's time to show this world the love in our hearts rather than the discontent that derives from our fear.

Whenever I'm speaking, I commonly hear that many of us are afraid to do something because we've never done it before. I get that. It's perfectly normal to be afraid of the unknown. As a college student I occasionally find myself fearful of the future, because I do not know what to expect after graduation. The fact is we all experience fear at some point in our lives, but we cannot let that fear stop us from fearlessly impacting our schools, businesses, communities and world. There is a thrill that comes with living fearlessly because it requires us to be in uncommon in our actions. Fearless leaders will stand out because it breaks the social barriers in a fear-filled world.

When I saw my sister take that jump, she displayed a characteristic that has sadly become a rare trait in our world and that trait is courage. Do you want to know the cure to drastically changing our world for the better? It starts by being courageous, vigilant, and most importantly, fearless. It's going against the odds, and despite precedence, doing the thing that's never been done before. There has never been a more perfect time to stand up, be **adventurous**, and **lead fearlessly** for the sake of making a positive, uplifting, and live-changing impact than this very moment. Remember this:

If there is no standard, then be the standard.

If there is no dream, then be the dreamer.

If there is no tradition, then start the tradition.

It's time to be bold and inspire courage.

It's time to be brave and let nothing hold you back.

It's time to be fearless by leaving the solace of the shallow to make a difference in the deep!

CAUGHT UP: Have you ever been so afraid of something it prevented you from doing something else? What was it and how did you overcome this fear?

CALLED OUT: How can you inspire those around you to be adventurous and live fearlessly?

What Do You Think?

_____

_____

_____

_____

_____

_____

_____

Chapter 5

Ambassadorship:
LIGHT IT UP & LET IT GO

A few months ago, I was driving by a high school football field and saw the players getting ready for a much anticipated year, but beyond the football players practice, you couldn't help but overhear the shouts of the cheerleading practice that was happening right across the street. As I listened to what the cheerleaders were chanting, I realized that they were doing a familiar cheer that we've all heard before. It went like this: "Let's Get Fired Up! Clap, clap, clap, clap, clap." Over and over again, the cheerleaders kept practicing this chant, with each cheer getting louder and each motion becoming more precise.

As I heard this, my mind went back and thought of two particular things. The first is when I use to play basketball in high school, every game our cheerleaders would do this chant and as a player it was indeed encouraging to hear. They were trying to get people excited, pumped, enthused, and, yes, pardon the pun, "Fired Up" about what could happen next for our team. The idea was that if everyone got involved, enough people would get fired up and began to really root for the team. The fans then could positively impact the atmosphere and ultimately help our team get a win! They felt like they had a responsibility to helping our team be all we could be.

When we look at life, it seems like many people are looking for a win. They're in a game, a game called life; a game that shows no mercy, a game that is brutal, it's unfair and often times we're up against the odds. But when life knocks us down, we must be willing to get back up. Just like the fans at the game, we as leaders have the opportunity to impact the atmosphere. We have the opportunity to make or break someone's day, an opportunity to make a difference in someone's life. We need to be excited about what will happen next, to get others involved and say the words "Let's Get Fired Up" to a very dry, cold, and desolate world. That choice starts with each of us.

I began to think of the words "Fired Up". Sure, we get fired up about football games, cookouts, museums, TV shows, competitions, food eating contests, among many other things. But, in this life, what does it mean to be completely fired up about something? When I think about the two words: "fired up", the first thing that comes to mind is a torchbearer. Before there were flashlights and even electricity, there were people who would carry torches of fire and light the way for the people to see, because if anyone was fired up back then, it was these guys, literally. They would guide, direct, and lead people into the right direction.

I went to my dictionary to see what the word torchbearer actually meant verbatim, it gave me this golden definition, The American Heritage Dictionary defines it as: "Torchbearer: One, such as the leader..., who imparts knowledge, truth, or inspiration to others."(www. ahdictionary.com) I want to ask you a question, "By this definition, are you a torchbearer?" Ambassadorship is all about representing yourself in a way that positively reflects the organization and people you symbolize.

Leaders are ambassadors, they light the way for others to follow. They represent something bigger than themselves and help model the way to live. There is nothing I crave more than to be a person who impacts others with truth, knowledge, and inspiration daily. There are people in our schools, communities, and in our own lives who are looking for guidance, direction, and leadership, we must ask ourselves, "Will we be the person that is willing to take the torch and lead the way?" Each of us have a fire that burns within us, a fire of influence that can inspire, motivate, and impact others in a positive way, but for what purpose will this fire of influence burn for? We must remember that though some people are silent, their hearts are crying out for a friend, will we be that friend?

In this dark world, so many people are looking for the light, a fire of inspiration, if you will, when in truth, we as the leaders are the ones who are holding the flame. As ambassadors of leadership, we must desire to be fired up, we must be caught up, but not just about the material things, but rather about the impact we can make on someone's life. We must be the "torchbearers" and carry the flame into today's dark world, people who burn with passion, model the way, believe in the future of this generation, and share their spark. This spark starts at the heart.

So no matter what you're starting, whether its school, college, a new job, a hobby, or even starting retirement, please know that each day is an opportunity where we can impact our atmosphere, we can positively influence someone's life, and we can ultimately change our world. We must always remember to be a friend, to fuel the flame. Be the spark. Be motivated. Be influential and be the "Torchbearer" we were meant to be.

As ambassadors we must become passionately fired up and excited about the future. Stoke your passion and light it up so much that it becomes a wildfire that will spread into the hearts of your followers. We do this not only by the words we say, but by focusing on our actions and understanding our choices have great implications. What we do, say, and promote is contagious and has a direct reflection on the things we represent. As an ambassador we have a duty to light it up; a mandate to set a good example for others to follow, but as much as we light it up, we also must learn to be people who help others let it go.

If you are like the majority of Americans, then I'm sure you're aware of Disney's movie "Frozen". I have seen this movie twice; once when my 9-year old sister begged me to take here to see it, so I opened the freezer door and showed her Frozen! Then, I watched the real thing with my family at the movies. The one thing that I took away from the movie and has yet to leave my mind is the song "Let It Go." The song about a queen who feels alone and ostracized because of her uncontrollable abilities has exploded with popularity. However, it's been on my heart to share with you a different side of this song that the marketing department at Disney won't share with you.

In the opening verses of the song, Queen Elsa sings that "she's in a Kingdom of Isolation and it looks like I'm the Queen." Almost all the places I speak at, I've realized a constant theme I hear from students, it's the belief that they feel like they are alone and no one cares about them. Many people tend to think they are alone because of their imperfections, their differences, & their home life. They feel alone because no one will reach out to them and tell them that they are worth something. They truly feel "FROZEN" in this world. Many even literally live out the line of "Conceal, don't feel, don't let them know", because they feel desolate and alone.

In my own life, I have found that hurt coincides with silence, many people are quiet on the outside, but inside their hearts are crying out to be part of something, to belong, and to feel empowered. But there is hope found in those who answer the call and are willing to reach out to others. Every person whether they know it or not has an influence and with that, you have the opportunity to impact a life for the better. Did you know that just by putting a positive status on Facebook or Twitter can make a difference? I was startled to find that over 75% of public school fights are now inspired by at least 1 negative post or comment on social media. In fact, the #1 school issue in America, isn't drugs, chewing gum, bad academics, teen drinking, or pregnancy, the top issue is BULLYING.

What we can gather from all this is that by looking purely at the issues facing today, they cannot be resolved by administrators, lawmakers, or school boards. No, the people who can resolve these issues are those who walk down the hallways of our schools every day and witness the issues first hand. Students, leaders who desire for something more for their school cultures can make the biggest difference in resolving these problems because they have a direct impact on the environment of their school. Imagine how much different our world would be if we just stopped, and decided to sit by the unpopular kids at lunch. The ones who are often disconnected from others; everyone no matter where they are at need to be reached out to. What would happen if we reached out and showed sincere care to the people we don't even know? What could happen if we gave a hurting person a shoulder to cry on and whisper the words "Let it Go" to them? What if we let all our pride and arrogance go and decided to change our generation regardless of what the "cool kids" think? Everyone matters.

I have a challenge for anyone who reads this book: let's bring the heat to our generation. Unlike Frozen's Queen Elsa, people don't have to feel frozen, because they're not alone. Be the leader who goes above the norm, by challenging the status quo, and breaking the proverbial "ICE". Reach out to others, give a smile to a smile less person, and be a friend to the friendless. The frozen truth is the fact that anyone can have an IMPACT on this world, but only if we're willing to believe in it and do it. Bottom line: Be the leader who FREEZES fear and MELTS mediocrity. Ambassadors, it's time for us to LIGHT IT UP and LET IT GO!

CAUGHT UP: If someone was to analyze your life for a week, what would be some of the leadership lessons they would learn from you?

CALLED OUT: As an ambassador, what can you do to be a positive example for others to follow?

What Do You Think?

_____

_____

_____

_____

_____

_____

_____

Chapter 6

Acknowledge:
"FINISH LAST"

I n this chapter, I'm excited to introduce to you another area of leadership called acknowledgement. My hope is that you will act upon the knowledge you have read in this book. So many times we utilize resources, we attend leadership conferences and trainings, we read leadership books, and we talk about how we want to be an effective leader. Although we may know who we are and what we can do, if we fail to acknowledge the needs of others, if we fail to acknowledge the true content of our hearts, if we fail to acknowledge the fact that we need to act upon our knowledge in order to impact, then we have missed out on what could have been and all of our efforts would be for nothing.

In order for us to be effective servant leaders, we must acknowledge action in our hearts. We must activate ourselves by applying what we know to what we can do for others. True service is equipped with passion and influence. When we acknowledge others first, we begin to put others as a priority. Leadership is all about getting behind people and propelling them forward into their destiny. Make others the priority by acknowledging the heart of service that is dwelling within you. In many cases this isn't easy, in fact, if life on earth was a race, servant leaders would not necessarily be first, we would be last.

When spring is in full swing, the weather being somewhat consistent, and allergies flaring (mine included), it's the perfect time of year to start running. That's right, across high schools, college campuses, and everywhere in between, you'll find people who run for fun. Runners have stamina in their bones, and legs that often feel like jelly. What once was everyone's only way of transportation has now become one of America's favorite hobbies, sports, and exercises. As a lifelong asthmatic, many would've never guessed that I ran Cross Country in high school. My senior year I remember running against some of the best runners in the state and I envied their ability to accomplish so much within such short amounts of times. They were naturally good runners that could excel with little practice, whereas, people like me had to literally run our tails off just to be somewhat competitive.

During my time, I was often asked what the crazy motives behind running so much were. The fact is I enjoyed running, and going into it, I knew I wasn't going to be the best one out there. In truth, the very first time I competed at a meet, I came in DEAD LAST. No joke. For me, it was about working hard by physically contributing to a team that I believed in. Eventually I was able to condition myself to the point where I was able to be competitive, but there was more to the story. Now, don't get me wrong, I would've loved to have been able to achieve a medal in cross country, but the ultimate success didn't come from the pursuit of a medal. The true rewards came from the experience of building my stamina, increasing my body's endurance, and developing my dedication and character to the team. If you were to summarize all the rewards into one phrase, it would be coined as personal growth.

I tend to think that in life, every one of us can be characterized as a runner. We all have goals, dreams, and ambitions that we shoot for, but we must keep our perspectives and motives in check. There are 2 different types of runners in our world: people who are running from their fears, and then there are people who are sprinting toward their future.

In our society, we put emphasis on the Super Bowl wins, the leadership roles, the champion livestock, the Academy Award nominations, the trophies, the finish line, and winning records. But the truth of the matter is that while these things are great accomplishments, these accolades don't last. They fade away just as the sun fades into the night. We're only on this planet for a short time and that should motivate us to do something that is lasting and memorable. And you may say, "Brandon, how do you do that?" Let me answer that question by asking YOU another question, "If you are a runner of life then what are you competing for?"

Many people are competing for the titles, but fewer are truly competing for the impact. Power hungry leaders care about their own benefit, but servant-minded leaders care about the benefit of others. Simply put: selfishness breeds destruction, but selflessness breeds restoration. Without a shadow of doubt, I can promise you that people will be far more motivated to respond to a selfless leader who leads by the heart, rather than by a title.

I will be very frank with you: there are so many people in this world who are hungry for a difference, craving for a change, and starving for an impact. The question is who will feed them? People's lives are waiting to be changed; and the future of their success depends on your choice to leave the impact on them by running your race strong! In this world's eyes, servant leaders may finish last, but that's because we desire to achieve something that is far greater than 1st place at the finish line. We finish last because we are tired of the norm and dream of shattering the negative statistics of our generation. We finish last because we don't seek power, we seek peace. We finish last, because we know that we run a race that is bigger than ourselves. I have a question for you, "Do you want to make a difference in the lives of others?" "Do you want to impact your generation in a very profound and lasting way?" "Are you willing to put yourself last, so that others may be first to experience your impact?' If you do, then I challenge you to RUN YOUR RACE like never before, work hard, make the most of it, put others above yourself, reach out to people, kick your heart in gear, love the unlovable, be a servant, compete for the difference, shift your focus beyond the finish line, beyond the material things, sprint toward your future, and begin to put your sights on making your IMPACT a reality. Be caught up in the pursuit of impact. Be available. Be authentic. Be an influential ambassador. Lastly, be the servant leader who acknowledges others first for this is where the heart of true servant leadership awaits. My name is Brandon Baumgarten and I have already decided to finish last. The question is, "Will you?"

CAUGHT UP: What has been the biggest leadership lesson you have learned from this book?

CALLED OUT: How will you use what you have learned to maximize your impact as a servant leader?

What Are Your Thoughts?

_____

_____

_____

_____

_____

_____

_____

_____

Chapter 7

Abandon:
LEAVING SELF BEHIND

"A ship is safe in harbor, but that's not what
ships are for."- William G.T. Shedd

I n our final chapter, we will be focusing on an aspect of servant leadership that is often talked about but can be one of the most challenging to apply from day to day. This lesson of servant leadership is called selflessness. As we have established earlier in the book, leadership is all about putting others first and pushing them forward to their destiny. Unfortunately, it would seem that our world gets this part mixed up mainly because many believe that leadership roles equate to superiority or being above others rather than beneath them. It's a sad state that resembles a ship that is made to achieve greatness, but is comfortable at the harbor, so it stays where there is no risk and no purpose to live out. The point is the ship was not created to simply absorb space and exist in the pure safety of a harbor. The ship was made to take on the task, to set the sail, and to weather the waves.

My belief is that there are so many of us who can relate to this analogy. Many have found themselves in a proverbial harbor of comfort, complacency, and apathy. All these factors lead to selfishness where we become so concerned about ourselves that we forget about everyone else. Servant leadership demands that we shift our focus from our selfish mindsets and push forward to focus on how we can serve one another. In this "me" centered society and entitlement-crazy generation, we must abandon ourselves; we must leave the shore of self by entering the new waters. We were not born to get, we were born to give.

I know this is easier said than done, but I understand being on the ship of self personally and it coincides with one of the first stories I shared with you in this book. If you recall in Chapter 1, I told you about my experience in running for National FFA Office. I'll never forget the long walk from the convention center to my hotel room. No doubt about it, the emotional, mental, and physical fatigue had hit me all it once.

When I made it back to my room, I fell onto my bed and allowed any emotion left within me to flow through my eyes. I was completely and utterly empty. I had no idea why I had fallen short of my goal, but it happened and for the days following this, I found myself wallowing on the ship of self. But what I didn't mention to you earlier was the other side of the story.

When I arrived back in Oklahoma, I was greeted by my parents, family, mentors, and former teammates with encouragement and support. Even though I had fallen short of achieving national office, they still believed in me and their support meant more than words can describe in a single book. I will never forget getting a phone call from the local Ag-Ed instructor at Oilton High School asking me to come and present a public speaking workshop at the school just days after returning back. He told me he thought it would help me get out of my slump, so I agreed to come, got in my car and headed to the school.

What would happen next would leave a huge impression on my life. As I turned on the road to head to the school, I began to notice some interaction ahead of me. Before my eyes, classes of elementary kids start racing towards my car, they had posters, confetti, balloons; they were jumping up and down, whooping and hollering with smiles on their faces. As I drove further I could see the middle and high school students doing the same thing. The teachers, staff, faculty, and people all from my hometown had met there and were celebrating my return.

Getting out of my car and looking at those around me, I couldn't help but scratch my head and think to myself, "These people are acting like I just won the Super Bowl, but the fact is, I lost. Why would they be happy about this outcome?" I quickly remembered that this adventure, this whole experience was never about me, but it was about those around me. You see, I was so caught up in my own failure that I forgot about the bigger picture. In that moment, I had to abandon myself realizing the smiles, the joy, and all the renewed school spirit I saw in the eyes of the people who were present that day in Oilton, Oklahoma. In the end, this journey was never about me, this book was not written for me, this life we live was never meant for just us. All of these efforts were made for others. Because this is what life is all about; this is what leadership is all about. Abandoning our own selfishness to help others is what we've been called to do and the result is a positive impact we can make on one another's lives.

When we become selfless, we better prepare ourselves to serve. In order to be effective leaders, we must leave self behind and understand that the real purpose begins when we put others first. Think about this: you may be the only positive influence someone will ever have in their life, let us labor in being that influence by excusing our selfishness, rolling up our sleeves, and putting forth the unselfish heart of service that results in legacy, impact, and a difference made. Empty your heart, leave self behind and lead with passion and I have no doubt you will have an explosive impact. We must be bold in our belief that we can impact others and be determined to see that the dawning of a new day brings another opportunity to set aside ourselves and help those around us to feel their true worth.

Looking ahead, the future of leaders has never been brighter than now and it's all in the hands of you and me. Let us never forget that each of us must be caught up in our purpose and understand that we have been called out to leave an impact on this world. This book, however, is useless if not applied to your life for it is your choice what you do with it. True impact is waiting on us and now more than ever we need leaders to respond.

Together, we can make a positive difference in our homes, classrooms, and world by bringing out the leader in each of us. Always remember that you were made to make a difference, you were meant to make a change, but most importantly, you were born to make an impact, the question is, "What impact will you leave behind?"

CAUGHT UP: Share a time you put someone else before yourself. What was the effect and how did it impact you?

CALLED OUT: How can you challenge yourself to be selfless in a selfish world?

What Are Your Thoughts?

_____

_____

_____

_____

_____

_____

_____

NOTES

Thanks for reading "Caught Up & Called Out" and congrats on finishing the book. I hope this resource has helped bring out the leader in you. Please feel free to refer this book to a friend or you can even write a review of it on Amazon or Facebook. If you are looking for a speaker at your next event, you can reach Brandon using the following information. **Keep the fire alive!**

Brandon Baumgarten

"Engage. Encourage. Empower."

Professional Speaker/Contributing Writer/ Leadership Coach

www.brandonbaumgarten.com

Printed in the United States
By Bookmasters